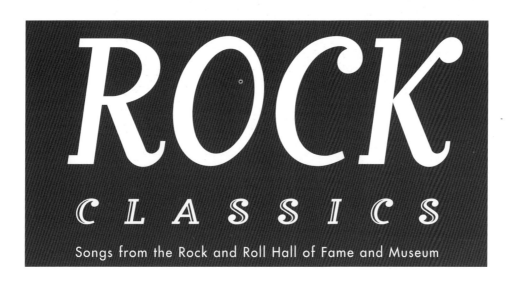

ROCK
CLASSICS
Songs from the Rock and Roll Hall of Fame and Museum

GW00758561

Universe

The Rock and Roll Hall of Fame

Leaders in the music industry joined together in 1983 to establish the Rock and Roll Hall of Fame Foundation. One of the Foundation's many goals and functions is to recognize the contributions of those who have had a significant impact over the evolution, development and perpetuation of rock and roll, by inducting them into the Hall of Fame.

There are three categories of inductees:

Performers:
Artists become eligible for induction 25 years after the release of their first record.

Non-Performers:
Songwriters, producers, disc jockeys, record executives, journalists, and others who had an impact on the development of rock and roll.

Early Influences:
Artists whose music predated rock and roll, but who inspired rock's leading artists and helped in the evolution of rock.

The Foundation's nominating committee, composed of rock and roll historians, selects nominees each year in the Performer category. Ballots are sent to an international voting body of about 1,000 rock experts. Those performers who receive the highest number of votes, and more than 50% of the vote, are inducted. The Foundation generally inducts five to seven performers each year.

The nominating committee annually elects the inductees in the Non-Performer and Early Influence categories.

Photo credits:
front cover: Jerry Lee Lewis, photo courtesy of Showtime Archives, Toronto; Aretha Franklin and Fats Domino, Archive Photos/Frank Driggs Collection; Janis Joplin, Michael Ochs Archives, Venice, Calif.
pp. 6, 28, 36, 38, 44, 64, 73, 74: Michael Ochs Archives, Venice, Calif.
pp. 10, 43, 70, 80: Archive Photos / Frank Driggs Collection
pp. 12, 24, 58: Courtesy of Showtime Archives, Toronto
pp. 16, 20: Archive Photos
p. 32: © 1994 Bob Gruen / Star File
p. 44: © Ed Thrasher / Michael Ochs Archives, Venice, Calif.
p. 53: © Terence Spencer, Retna / Camera Press
p. 54: REX USA LTD.
p. 62: © Elliott Landy

Published in the United States of America in 1997 by
UNIVERSE PUBLISHING
A Division of Rizzoli International Publications, Inc.
300 Park Avenue South
New York, NY 10010

97 98 99 00 01 / 10 9 8 7 6 5 4 3 2 1

Library of Congress catalog card number 97-60761

Design by Danton Mayorga
Music engraved by Hal Leonard Corporation

Printed in Italy

CONTENTS

Introduction

This book is a tribute to the great *songs* of rock and roll. Though there are many elements that contribute to the music—look, style, attitude, rhythm, and so on—in the end what most of us remember about the best rock and roll are the songs, from the brilliant two- and three-minute classics that were ready-made for the car radio, to the longer, more intricate jams of the late sixties and seventies, to the lyrically astute songs of protest and the singer-songwriter movements.

All of the songs in this book were recorded by Rock and Roll Hall of Fame inductees, artists who have created a substantial body of work over the course of lengthy—and legendary—careers. Though all of these people have recorded numerous songs worthy of inclusion, the selection here is a representative sample of classic songs from different eras, from the fifties to the seventies. (Because of eligibility rules, the Hall of Fame has not yet inducted artists whose careers began after the early seventies.)

Two of the songs are anthems that emerged from producer Sam Phillips's Sun Studio in the mid-fifties: Carl Perkins's "Blue Suede Shoes" and Jerry Lee Lewis's "Great Balls of Fire." Elvis Presley's breakthrough hit for RCA Records, "Heartbreak Hotel," is here, as is Little Richard's first smash, "Tutti Frutti." Along with Hank Ballard's "The Twist," Fats Domino's "Blueberry Hill" and Willie Dixon's "I'm Your Hoochie Coochie Man," these songs formed the foundation upon which rock and roll was built.

In the sixties, rock and roll exploded in many directions. The British Invasion brought artists like the Beatles and the Who to the U.S. "She Loves You," released in 1964, was the Beatles's second Number One single in America and a terrific example of the band's well-honed rock and roll chops. "I Can See for Miles" came out in 1967, during the Summer of Love, and was the Who's first Top Ten hit stateside. Around that time, a second generation of British-based artists, heavily influenced by the burgeoning psychedelic movement, emerged. Cream's "The Sunshine of Your Love" is a touchstone of that period.

American music also prospered during the sixties. The Drifters carried on the great vocal-group tradition that began in the fifties; "Under the Boardwalk" is one of the many standout songs the group recorded for Atlantic Records. Rhythm & blues also continued to play a key role in the development of rock and roll. The Isley Brothers's "Twist and Shout" not only was a hit for them; the Beatles, heavily influenced by American music, also scored with the song.

Up in Detroit, Berry Gordy Jr. was creating what he called the Sound of Young America on the Motown label, and the Supremes were the most successful female group of the era. They took "You Keep Me Hangin' On" to the top of the charts in November 1966. Two years later, Vanilla Fudge gave the song a psychedelic overhaul, and it again

The Inductees

1986	1987	1988	1989	1990	1991
Chuck Berry	The Coasters	The Beach Boys	Dion	Hank Ballard	LaVern Baker
James Brown	Eddie Cochran	The Beatles	Otis Redding	Bobby Darin	The Byrds
Ray Charles	Bo Diddley	The Drifters	The Rolling	The Four Seasons	John Lee Hooker
Sam Cooke	Aretha Franklin	Bob Dylan	Stones	The Four Tops	The Impressions
Fats Domino	Marvin Gaye	The Supremes	The Temptations	The Kinks	Wilson Pickett
The Everly	Bill Haley		Stevie Wonder	The Platters	Jimmy Reed
Brothers	B. B. King	**Non-Performer**		Simon and	Ike and Tina
Buddy Holly	Clyde McPhatter	Berry Gordy	**Non-Performer**	Garfunkel	Turner
Jerry Lee Lewis	Rick Nelson		Phil Spector	The Who	
Elvis Presley	Roy Orbison	**Early Influences**			**Non-Performers**
Little Richard	Carl Perkins	Woody Guthrie	**Early Influences**	**Non-Performers**	Dave
	Smokey Robinson	Lead Belly	The Ink Spots	Gerry Goffin and	Bartholomew
Non-Performers	Big Joe Turner	Les Paul	Bessie Smith	Carole King	Ralph Bass
Alan Freed	Muddy Waters		The Soul Stirrers	Holland, Dozier	
Sam Phillips	Jackie Wilson			and Holland	**Early Influence**
					Howlin' Wolf
Early Influences	**Non-Performers**			**Early Influences**	
Robert Johnson	Leonard Chess			Louis Armstrong	**Lifetime**
Jimmie Rodgers	Ahmet Ertegun			Charlie Christian	**Achievement**
Jimmy Yancey	Jerry Leiber and			Ma Rainey	Nesuhi Ertegun
	Mike Stoller				
Lifetime	Jerry Wexler				
Achievement					
John Hammond	**Early Influences**				
	Louis Jordan				
	T-Bone Walker				
	Hank Williams				

became a hit. Meanwhile, under the guidance of producer Jerry Wexler, Atlantic Records was helping create a new type of African-American music, called soul. Aretha Franklin was its queen, and "A Natural Woman," included here, reached the Top Ten in 1967. The song was written by the Brill Building team of Carole King and Gerry Goffin, Hall of Fame inductees themselves.

In Los Angeles, the Byrds combined the pop sensibility of the Beatles with the lyric content of the folk movement. "Turn! Turn! Turn!" was their second hit, its lyrics adapted by folk legend (and Hall of Famer) Pete Seeger from the Book of Ecclesiastes. The Byrds would go on to score one of the first psychedelic hits, "Eight Miles High," as well as help invent country-rock. The Band, a group of four Canadians and one American, started out as the backing group for rockabilly artist Ronnie Hawkins. After a stint with Bob Dylan, they holed up in Woodstock and recorded *Music from Big Pink*, an album that, like the work of the Byrds, helped move rock and roll in a more roots-oriented direction. "The Weight" was one of that album's gems.

Another icon of the sixties was Janis Joplin. "Me and Bobby McGee," written by Kris Kristofferson, was her only Number One hit. Unfortunately, it reached that peak a few months after her death.

Three of the most influential artists of the seventies are also included here: Bob Marley, whose "I Shot the Sheriff" was a major hit for Hall of Fame inductee Eric Clapton; John Lennon, with "Imagine," and Pink Floyd with "Money."

Each of these songs has its own unique genesis, and each artist approaches song writing in his or her own way. But in the end, a terrific performance of remarkable song is what makes rock and roll magical. All of the songs herein undeniably lend themselves to such a performance.

James Henke
Chief Curator
Rock and Roll Hall of Fame and Museum
Cleveland, Ohio

1992	**1993**	**1994**	**1995**	**1996**	**1997**
Bobby "Blue" Bland	Ruth Brown	The Animals	The Allman Brothers Band	David Bowie	The Bee Gees
Booker T. and the MGs	Cream	The Band	Al Green	Gladys Knight and the Pips	Buffalo Springfield
Johnny Cash	Creedence Clearwater Revival	Duane Eddy	Janis Joplin	Jefferson Airplane	Crosby, Stills and Nash
Jimi Hendrix Experience	The Doors	The Grateful Dead	Led Zeppelin	Little Willie John	The Jackson 5
Isley Brothers	Etta James	Elton John	Martha and the Vandellas	Pink Floyd	Joni Mitchell
Sam and Dave	Frankie Lymon and the Teenagers	John Lennon	Neil Young	The Shirelles	Parliament-Funkadelic
The Yardbirds	Van Morrison	Bob Marley	Frank Zappa	The Velvet Underground	The (Young) Rascals
	Sly and the Family Stone	Rod Stewart			

1992
Non-Performers
Leo Fender
Bill Graham
Doc Pomus

Early Influences
Elmore James
Professor Longhair

1993
Non-Performers
Dick Clark
Milt Gabler

Early Influence
Dinah Washington

1994
Non-Performer
Johnny Otis

Early Influence
Willie Dixon

1995
Non-Performer
Paul Ackerman

Early Influence
The Orioles

1996
Non-Performer
Tom Donahue

Early Influence
Pete Seeger

1997
Non-Performer
Syd Nathan

Early Influences
Bill Monroe
Mahalia Jackson

Blue Suede Shoes

Words and Music by
CARL LEE PERKINS

Bright tempo (not too fast)

Well, it's one for the mon-ey, two for the show, three to get read-y, now

go, cat, go but don't you step on my blue suede shoes. You can

do an-y-thing but lay off of my blue suede shoes. Well, you can

knock me down, step on my face, slan-der my name all o-ver the place;
burn my house, steal my car, drink my ci-der from my old fruit jar;

N.C.   F7

Do an-y-thing that you want to do, __ but uh - uh, hon-ey, lay off of my shoes. __

Bb7   3   F   F

Don't you   step on my blue suede shoes.   You can

C   Bb   1.   F   Bb7

do an - y - thing __ but lay off of my blue suede shoes.

F   C   N.C.   2.   F   Bb7   F   F7#9

Well you can shoes. _____

Carl Perkins • inducted 1987

Carl Perkins is one of the fathers of rockabilly. His songs and inimitable vocal and guitar style are among the finest examples of a genre that pulled together some of the most potent sounds of the South: country, blues, and rock and roll. Along with such pioneers as Johnny Cash, Jerry Lee Lewis, and Elvis Presley, Perkins was an alumnus of Sun Records in Memphis.

Perkins released his classic "Blue Suede Shoes" in 1956; a huge hit for its composer, the song also became one of Elvis Presley's hallmarks after he cut his own version later that year. Other superstars would pay tribute to Perkins by recording his material: during the early sixties, the Beatles released versions of "Everybody's Trying to Be My Baby," "Honey Don't," and Perkins's adaptation of the blues, "Matchbox." Among the countless artists significantly influenced by Perkins's rockabilly style are George Harrison, Paul McCartney, John Fogerty, Dave Edmunds, and Brian Setzer (of Stray Cats fame).

Blueberry Hill

Words and Music by AL LEWIS,
LARRY STOCK and VINCENT ROSE

Gm   D7   G   Bb7 Eb7 Ab

_____ were nev - er to be. _____ Tho' we're a - part, _____

_____ you're part of me still _____ for you were my

Bb7   Eb   Ab6   Ebmaj7

thrill _____ on Blue-ber - ry Hill.

Fats Domino • inducted 1986

Antoine "Fats" Domino is the big man of the Big Easy—New Orleans's number one hit maker. With his balmy piano rhythms and lolling vocals, Domino was already a familiar presence on the R&B charts by the early fifties. (His first hit, "The Fat Man," was a million-selling hit in 1949.) From 1955 to 1960, Domino—in collaboration with his producer and songwriting partner Dave Bartholomew—made history with a string of major-selling singles, including "Ain't That a Shame," "I'm Walkin'," "Blue Monday," "I'm In Love Again," and his adaptation of the twenties standard "Blueberry Hill." In 1968, the Beatles paid tribute to Fats with "Lady Madonna," which borrowed Domino's trademark piano and vocal style. Having once boasted in song that he was "ready, willing, and able to rock and roll all night," Fats has been proving he's a man of his word by for more than forty years.

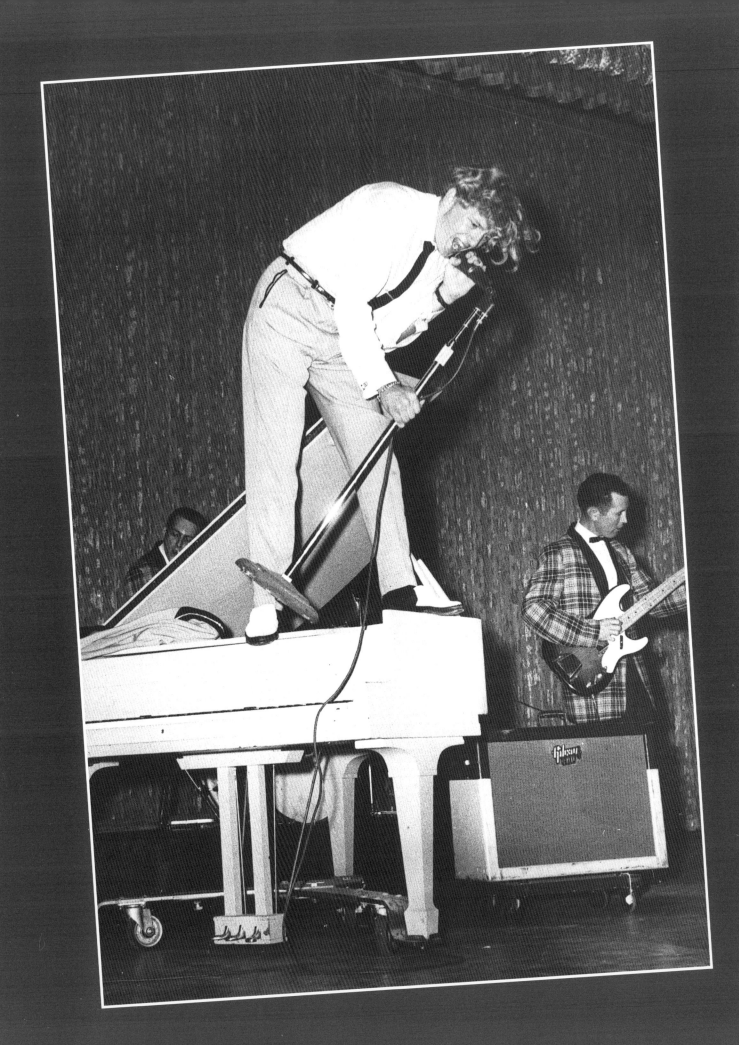

Great Balls of Fire

Words and Music by OTIS BLACKWELL
and JACK HAMMER

love's just fine. _ Good - ness gra - cious, great _ balls of fire!

Instrumental ends

Kiss me, ba - by. Woo, _____ it feels good.

Hold me, ba - by. { Girl, just let me love you like a lov-er should. _
I want to love you like a lov-er should. _ }

You're fine, _ so kind, _ I'm gon-na tell the world that you're mine, mine, mine, mine. _

I chew my nails and I twid-dle my thumb. _ I'm real ner-vous but it sure is fun. _

14

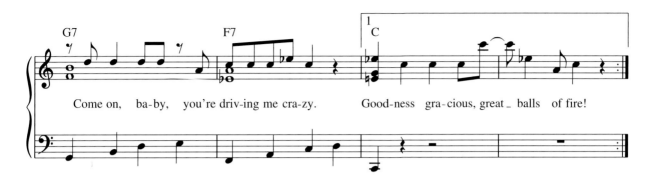

Come on, ba-by, you're driv-ing me cra-zy. Good-ness gra-cious, great _ balls of fire!

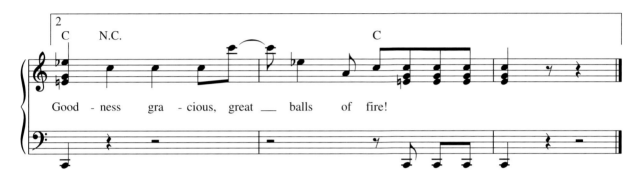

Good - ness gra - cious, great ___ balls of fire!

Jerry Lee Lewis • inducted 1986

Rockers have spent the last thirty years trying to top Jerry Lee Lewis as the music's wildest performer. Lewis came out of Memphis's Sun Records, part of a slew of influential talent that included Johnny Cash, Roy Orbison, Carl Perkins, and Elvis Presley. Two 1957 hits, "Whole Lotta Shakin' Going On" and "Great Balls of Fire," featuring his wild vocals and stomping piano, established Lewis as a rock and roll original. Subsequent high-voltage singles, "Breathless" and "High School Confidential," as well as a mounting reputation as the most exciting and unpredictable performer on the rock and roll circuit, seemed to point the way toward superstardom, but the first of a series of lifelong scandals—marrying his thirteen-year-old cousin—sidelined Lewis's career. Through it all, nothing has kept the piano-pounding wildman still for very long.

Heartbreak Hotel

**Words and Music by MAE BOREN AXTON,
TOMMY DURDEN and ELVIS PRESLEY**

Well, since my ___ ba-by left me, well I found a new place to dwell. Well it's

down at the end ___ of Lone-ly Street, that's Heart-break Ho-tel. I'll be, I'll be so lone-ly, ba-by.

Well, I'm so lone-ly. I'll be so lone-ly ___ I could die. Al -

though it's al - ways crowd-ed you still can find ___ some room for
bell-hop's tears ___ keep flow-ing and the desk clerk's dressed ___ in black. Well, they

bro - ken heart - ed lov - ers __ to cry there in the gloom. __ You'll be so,
been so long __ on Lone - ly Street they'll nev - er nev - er look back. It'll make you so

it'll make you so lone - ly, ba - by. It'll make you so lone - ly.
it'll make you so lone - ly, ba - by. Well, they're so lone - ly.

Oh, they're so lone - ly __ they could die. Now the
Oh, they're so lone - ly __ they could die. Well, now

if your __ ba - by leaves you and you've got a tale __ to tell, well just
Instrumental

take a walk __ down Lone - ly Street to Heart-break Ho - tel where you will be,

A7

you will be so lone - ly, ba - by. Well, you'll be lone - ly.

B7

1
E

2
E

D.S. al Coda

You'll be so lone - ly ____ you could die. Al -

CODA

E

F7 **E7**

die.

Elvis Presley • inducted 1986

They call him the King of Rock and Roll, for Elvis Presley is the man who put the music on the map. His international fame and record sales hit unprecedented heights for a popular performer, firmly establishing rock and roll as the defining sound of the late twentieth century. Elvis's rags-to-riches story has become part of American mythology. After Presley's discovery in 1954 by Sun Records producer Sam Phillips, the singer's upward trajectory was swift, direct, and seemingly unstoppable. Signed by RCA in 1956, Presley recorded "Heartbreak Hotel" (co-written by Mae Axton, singer/actor Hoyt Axton's mother), which became the first of a steady stream of Number One hits. Over the next two decades—complete with a stint in the Army, a film career, and dramatic concert appearances—Presley dominated rock and roll, selling millions of records and influencing untold numbers of future pop musicians. The luster of Elvis's glory days and his startling music have lost none of their magic and power.

The Who • inducted 1990

The Who are one of the principal architects of hard rock. Guitarist Pete Townshend, vocalist Roger Daltrey, drummer Keith Moon, and bassist John Entwistle galvanized the pop world during the British Invasion of the mid-sixties. Their brutally powerful sound and explosive live performances regularly ended in an orgy of destruction as Townshend and Moon demolished their instruments. Townshend's brilliant songcraft was firmly in place by 1968's *The Who Sell Out*, which featured the hit single "I Can See for Miles." A series of masterful albums followed, including 1969's pioneering rock opera *Tommy*, *Live at Leeds*, *Who's Next*, and *Quadrophenia*. (*Tommy* has since been adapted into a ballet, a film, and a Broadway musical.) Already legends by the time of Moon's death in 1978, the Who provided the blueprint for hundreds of loud-and-proud bands that followed in their path.

I Can See For Miles

Words and Music by
PETER TOWNSHEND

Bright Rock

I know you've de-ceived me. Now here's a sur-prise.

I know that you have 'cos there's ma-gic in ___ my eyes.

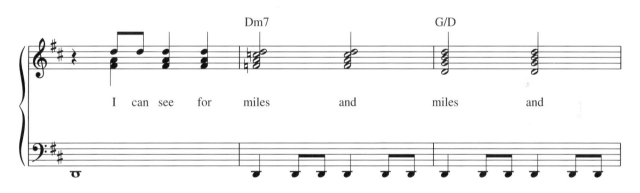

I can see for miles and miles and

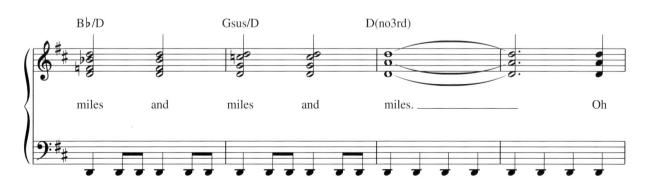

miles and miles and miles. ___ Oh

Willie Dixon • inducted 1994

Willie Dixon was both the finest composer and the most important behind-the-scenes recording man in modern blues history. As a songwriter, producer, talent scout, A&R supervisor, and bassist at Chess Records, Dixon worked with nearly every major Chicago blues artist of the post war era including Muddy Waters, Howlin' Wolf, Sonny Boy Williamson, and Little Walter—not to mention his early involvement with seminal rockers Chuck Berry and Bo Diddley. Dixon's songs still form the core of the blues repertoire: "I'm Your Hoochie Coochie Man," "I Ain't Superstitious," "The Seventh Son," "Back Door Man," "Little Red Rooster," "Spoonful," "I Just Wanna Make Love to You." These, and many other Dixon favorites, also made up the basic songbook of the sixties blues-rock movement, as recorded by such superstar groups as Cream, the Rolling Stones, Led Zeppelin, the Doors, the Jeff Beck Group, and the Allman Brothers Band. Near the end of his life, Dixon developed the Blues Heaven Foundation, an organization dedicated to the continuation of the music and to retrieving royalties and copyrights for blues artists.

I'm Your Hoochie Coochie Man

Written by
WILLIE DIXON

Solid beat

The gyp-sy wom-an told my moth-er,
I got a black cat's bone, ___
On the sev - enth hour, ___

be-fore I was born, ___
I got a mo-jo too, ___
and on the sev-enth day, ___

you got a boy-child com - ing,   he's
I'm John the Con - quer - or, ___
on the sev - enth month, ___   the

gon-na be a son-of-a   gun. ___
I'm gon-na mess with you. ___
sev - en doc - tors say. ___

He's gon-na make   pret-ty wom - en,   he's
I'm gon-na make you pret-ty girls _____
He was born ____ for good luck   and

gon - na make 'em jump and shout.
lead   me   by   the   hand.
that you're   gon - na   see.

Then the world could   know
Then the world will   know
I've got sev-en hun-dred dol-lars, ba-by,

what this was all a-bout. ___
I'm the hoo-chie coo-chie man. ___ Lord, __ I'm here, ___ oh yeah. __
don't you __ mess with me. ___

___ Ev-'ry-bod-y knows __ I'm here, __ oh Lord, _____ 'cause I'm a

hoo-chie coo-chie man. __ Ev-'ry-bod-y knows __ I'm here.

here. _____

I Shot the Sheriff

Words and Music by
BOB MARLEY

Moderately slow, with a beat

1. I shot the sher - iff, but I did not shoot the dep - u - ty.
2.-4. *(See additional lyrics)*

I shot the sher - iff, but I did-n't shoot the

dep-u-ty. All a-round in my home town, they're

try - ing to track me down. _____ They say they want to bring me in guilt-

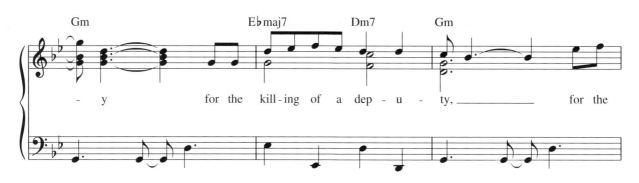

- y   for the kill-ing of a dep - u - ty, _____ for the

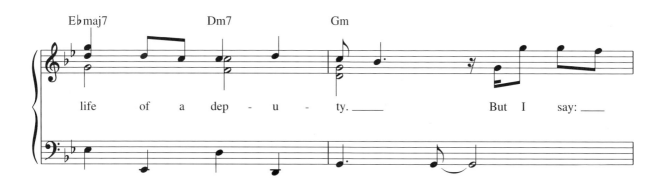

life   of   a   dep - u - ty. ____   But I   say: ____

Additional Lyrics

2. I shot the sheriff, but I swear it was in self-defense.
   I shot the sheriff, and they say it was a capital offense.
   Sheriff John Brown always hated me; for what, I don't know.
   Every time that I plant a seed, he said, "Kill it before it grows."
   He said, "Kill it before it grows." But I say:

3. I shot the sheriff, but I swear it was in self-defense.
   I shot the sheriff, but I swear it was in self-defense.
   Freedom came my way one day, and I started out of town.
   All of a sudden, I see sheriff John Brown aiming to shoot me down.
   So I shot, I shot him down. But I say:

4. I shot the sheriff, but I did not shoot the deputy.
   I shot the sheriff, but I did'nt shoot the deputy.
   Reflexes got the better of me, and what is to be must be.
   Every day, the bucket goes to the well, but one day the bottom will drop out.
   Yes, one day the bottom will drop out. But I say:

Bob Marley • inducted 1994

In his short lifetime Bob Marley became as famous across the world as any musician since Elvis Presley. Marley sang for the oppressed—be they in his native Jamaica, in Africa, or the inner cities of the U.S. With his original band, the Wailers, and then as a solo artist, he embodied the spirit of reggae, in all its syncopated, life-affirming glory.

Marley certainly didn't invent reggae or even devise his signature sound himself—his bandmates Peter Tosh and Bunny Wailer were integral to the process—but he mated an expansive social vision with an impassioned song-writing and performance style that elevated a regional sound into a world-wide phenomenon. His songs, including "No Woman No Cry," "Redemption Song," "Is This Love?" and "I Shot the Sheriff," told stories of opposition, liberation, and celebration. Marley may have died in 1981, but his songs, and their enduring message, are as vital as ever.

Imagine

Words and Music by
JOHN LENNON

tries. / sions.
It is-n't hard ___ to do. ___
I won-der if you ___ can. ___

Noth-ing to kill ___ or die _____ for / No need for greed ___ or hun - ger,
and no re - li - gion, ___ too. ___ / a broth-er-hood ___ of man. ___

Im-ag - ine all ___ the peo - ple ___ / Im-ag - ine all ___ the peo - ple ___

liv - ing ___ life in peace. ___ } / shar - ing ___ all the world. ___ }
You _____
you may say _____ I'm a

dream-er.
But I'm not the on - ly one. ___

F   G   C   E7   1   F   G

I hope some day ____ you'll join us ____   and the world ___ will

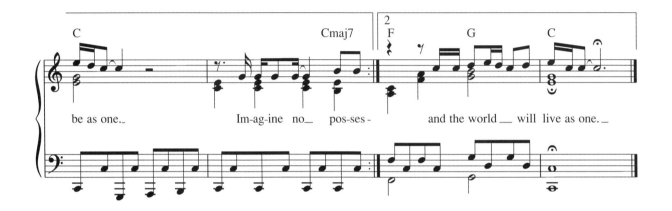

C   Cmaj7   2   F   G   C

be as one._   Im-ag-ine no_ pos-ses-   and the world ___ will live as one._

John Lennon • inducted 1994

John Lennon's tragic death in 1980 deprived the world of one of this century's most significant composers and performers— a socially conscious artist with a rare universal vision. Lennon's creative immortality was already assured from his work with the Beatles. The timeless songs he wrote for the group, both singularly and in collaboration with his partner Paul McCartney, are too numerous to mention. Embarking on a solo career in 1970—with wife Yoko Ono as his constant muse and sometime musical partner— Lennon continued to compose memorable songs, including "Instant Karma!," "Mother," "Working Class Hero," and "Watching the Wheels."

But few songs he wrote have had as lasting an impact as "Imagine," the 1971 title track of Lennon's second solo album. "Imagine" employs a simple, unadorned melody and plainspoken lyrics, but its forthright message of personal tolerance and worldwide peace resounds with a power mightier than any political rhetoric. A gift to a world that he left far too soon, "Imagine" keeps the creative genius and boundless humanity of Lennon with us still.

Me and Bobby McGee

Words and Music by KRIS KRISTOFFERSON
and FRED FOSTER

Moderately

Bust - ed flat in Bat - on Rouge, head - in' for the trains;
coal mines of Ken - tuck - y to the Cal - i - for - nia sun,

Feel-in' near - ly fad - ed as my jeans,_____ Bob - by thumbed a
Bob - by shared the se - crets of my soul;_____ Stand-in' right be -

die - sel down just be - fore it rained; Took us all the
side me, Lord, through ev - ery-thing I done, And ev - ery night she

way to New Or - leans._____ Then I took my har -
kept me from the cold._____ Then some-where near Sa -

poon out of my dir - ty, red ban - dan - na and was blow-in' sad while
lin - as, Lord, I let her slip a - way Look - in' for the

C7   **F**

Bob - by sang the blues; _____ With them wind-shield wi - pers
home I hope she'll find; _____ And I'd trade all of my to -

C   **G7**

slap - pin' time and Bob - by clap-pin' hands we fi - n'ly sang up ev - 'ry
mor - rows for a sin - gle yes - ter - day, hold - in' Bob - by's

C   **F**

song that driv - er knew. Free-dom's just an - oth - er word for
bod - y next to mine. Free-dom's just an - oth - er word for

G7

noth - in' left to lose, Noth-in' ain't worth noth - in', but it's
noth - in' left to lose, Noth-in' left is all she left for

free; _____
me; _____

Feel-in' good was eas - y, Lord, when

Bob-by sang the blues;

And feel-in' good was good e - nough for
And, bud-dy, that was good e - nough for

me, _____
me, _____

Good e-nough for me and Bob-by Mc -

1

Gee. _____

2

From the Gee. _____

Janis Joplin • inducted 1995

Janis Joplin sang as hard as she lived. There seemed to be little division between her life and her art; reveling in excessive pleasure or fighting her inner demons in public through song, Joplin's wrenching honesty was impossible not to respond to.

A transplanted Texan, she moved to San Francisco and hooked up with a raucous psychedelic band called Big Brother and the Holding Company. After an electrifying appearance at the 1967 Monterey Pop Festival, Big Brother signed with Columbia; a year later their debut album *Cheap Thrills* (with Joplin's legendary showstoppers "Piece of My Heart" and "Ball and Chain") became one of the year's top-selling albums. Going solo, Joplin adopted an earthier R&B feel on the two albums she completed before her death in 1971. *Pearl*, her final project, featured the posthumous Number One hit "Me and Bobby McGee," written by her former boyfriend Kris Kristofferson. The title of another song from *Pearl* perfectly captures the legendary singer's living-for-the-moment ethos: "Get It While You Can."

Money

Words and Music by
ROGER WATERS

prise that they're giv - ing none a - way. _____

Repeat and Fade

Pink Floyd • inducted 1996

Pink Floyd are the reigning champions of progressive rock. The original muse of this British quartet was Syd Barrett, the eccentric guitarist, vocalist, and songwriter whose whimsical experiments in musical psychedelia gave the band its early identity. With Barrett's departure in 1967, bassist Roger Waters gradually became the chief architect of the band's new sound. Their albums, including *Wish You Were Here* and *The Wall,* evolved into dense sonic landscapes that probed the psychological and social nightmares of a repressed society.

The epitome of that cheerless vision was *Dark Side of the Moon;* released in 1973, it remained on the U.S. charts for years, far outlasting any other recording in commercial longevity. The album's scathing hit single, "Money," with its memorable intro of rhythmic cash registers, has found a permanent home on FM radio stations. Although Waters departed in the late eighties, Pink Floyd lives on and prospers—proof that even fear, rage, and anxiety can be savored when expressed through the prisms of grand, visionary rock.

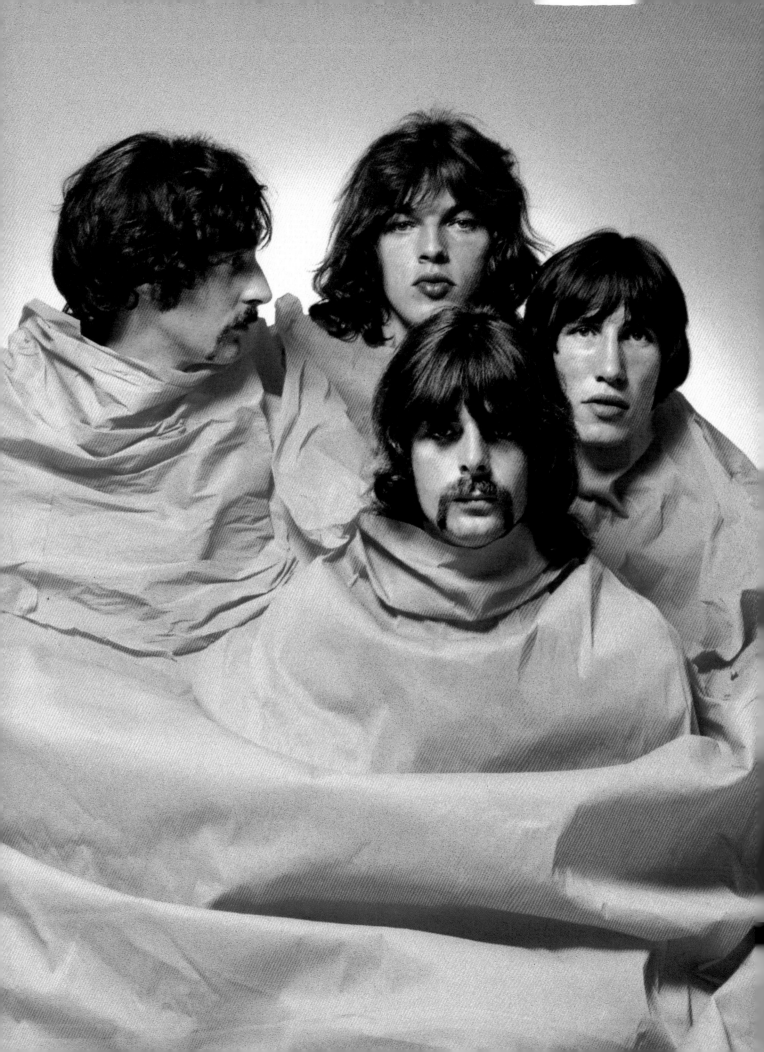

(You Make Me Feel Like)
A Natural Woman

Words and Music by GERRY GOFFIN,
CAROLE KING and JERRY WEXLER

life was so un-kind. Your love was the
of what I'm liv-ing for, 'cause if I make you hap - py

key to my ___ peace of mind, _____ } 'cause you make me___
I don't need to do ____ more, _____

feel, _____ you make me __ feel, _____ you make me __

feel like a ___ nat - u - ral wom-an.

Oh, __ ba - by, what you've done to me! _ (What you've done to me! ____)

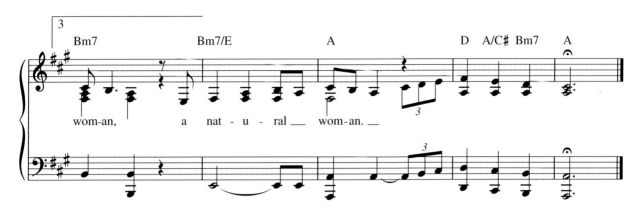

wom-an,   a   nat - u - ral __ wom-an. __

**Aretha Franklin
inducted 1987**

Dubbed the "Queen of Soul" in the late sixties, Aretha Franklin's title remains unchallenged. The daughter of a renowned preacher, Aretha grew up surrounded by such legends of gospel singing as Mahalia Jackson and Clara Ward. Franklin's immense talent was apparent by her teenage years; switching from gospel to pop music, she signed with Columbia Records in 1963. But it wasn't until she moved to Atlantic Records in late 1966 and aligned herself with producer Jerry Wexler that Franklin found a sympathetic recording environment. Wexler reconnected the singer to her gospel roots, and the ensuing fervor immediately revolutionized soul music. The producer also brought his star artist the best material he could find—the enduring "(You Make Me Feel Like) A Natural Woman" was written by the brilliant songwriting team of Carole King and Gerry Goffin. (Wexler commissioned the song by suggesting the title.)

After her Atlantic triumphs, Franklin settled into her role as the reigning diva of soul music. Whitney Houston, Mariah Carey, and every young up-and-comer who's ever followed in Franklin's footsteps pays explicit homage to her; they may be princesses, but she's still the queen.

Wild Thing

Words and Music by
CHIP TAYLOR

Moderately slow, with a beat

Wild Thing, you make my heart sing,

you make eve - ry thing groov - y.

Wild Thing.

Wild Thing, I ___
Wild Thing, I ___

___ think I love you.   But I wan - na know ___ for sure.
___ think you move me.   But I wan - na know ___ for sure.

Jimi Hendrix Experience • inducted 1992

There were rock guitarists before and after Jimi Hendrix, but no one so thoroughly transformed the nature of the instrument and the way it could be played as this brilliant radical. Hendrix paid his dues on the black music circuit throughout the early sixties, playing behind a host of top R&B stars including Little Richard and the Isley Brothers before he relocated to England in 1966 to form a group. The Jimi Hendrix Experience exploded on the British pop scene with their singles, "Hey Joe" and the psychedelic anthem "Purple Haze." The group's notorious live appearances featured the guitarist's flamboyant and frankly lascivious performance style. A winning appearance at the Monterey Pop Festival in 1967 broke the U.S. market wide open for the Experience. Hendrix completed only two more albums in his lifetime, yet each displayed advanced guitar work and innovative production. In the brief three years of fame before his untimely death in 1970, Hendrix gave the rock world more than enough to keep everyone busy well into the next millennium.

Ramblin' Man

Words and Music by
DICKEY BETTS

Lord, I was born a ram-blin' man, try'n' to make a liv-in' and do-in' the best I can. And when it's time for leav-in,' I hope you'll un-der-stand that I was born a ram-blin' man. Well, my

fa - ther was _ a gam - bler down in Geor - gia, _ and he
on my way _ to New _ Or - leans this morn - in', _

wound up on _ the wrong _ end of a gun. _ And
leav - in' out _ of Nash - ville, Ten - nes - see. _ They're

I was born _ in the back _ seat _ of a Grey - hound _ bus _
al - ways hav - in' a good time down _ on the bay - ou. Lord, _ them

roll - in' _ down High - way For - ty - one. _
del - ta wom - en think the world of me. _

Lord, I _ was born _ a ram - blin' man, _

try'n' to make a liv-in' and do-in' the best I _____ can. ___ And

when it's time ___ for leav - in', ___ I hope you'll un - der-stand _____

that I was born ___ a ram - blin' man.

I'm man.

The Allman Brothers Band
inducted 1995

The Allman Brothers Band originated progressive southern rock. Formed in early 1969, at all-night jam sessions in Jacksonville, Florida, the original group included lead and slide guitarist Duane Allman, his brother Gregg Allman on Hammond B-3 organ, lead guitarist Dickey Betts, bassist Berry Oakley, and drummers Butch Trucks and Jai Johanny Johanson (now known as Jaimoe). Mixing slashing blues-rock and long improvisatory jams, the "Brothers" were entering superstar status when Duane was killed in a motorcycle accident in 1971, followed by Berry a year later, also in a motorcycle accident. The group soldiered on, and with their 1973 album *Brothers and Sisters*, and with its hit single "Ramblin' Man," indeed became one of the top bands of the seventies. In their wake came the Marshall Tucker Band, Lynyrd Skynyrd, The Charlie Daniels Band, and a host of other popular southern rockers.

She Loves You

Words and Music by JOHN LENNON
and PAUL McCARTNEY

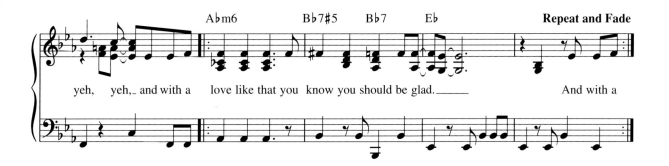

Abm6 Bb7#5 Bb7 Eb **Repeat and Fade**

yeh, yeh,_ and with a love like that you know you should be glad._____ And with a

The Beatles
inducted 1988

Is it possible to imagine rock and roll without the Beatles? Synthesizing everything that came before them, defining their contemporary era and subsequently influencing all that followed, the Beatles are, without question, the most important band in the music's history. That their pop culture revolution was accomplished in just eight short years—from 1962 to 1970—makes the achievement of John Lennon, Paul McCartney, George Harrison, and Ringo Starr that much more amazing.

The one-two punch of "I Want to Hold Your Hand" and "She Loves You" struck America hard in 1964; the group's vibrant harmonies and infectious energy coupled with Lennon and McCartney's refined songcraft, already evident on these early singles, brought a new vitality to popular music.

Rapid evolution and experimentation marked the next six years; their advances were closely monitored by every other rock artist. The band's golden age of artistic maturity began in late 1965 with *Rubber Soul*, continued with *Revolver*, and hit a peak with the 1967 masterpiece *Sgt. Pepper's Lonely Hearts Club Band*. *Abbey Road* (actually recorded after the sessions later released as their final album, *Let It Be*) revealed that despite internal dissension, the foursome was as innovative as ever. Nearly thirty years after their breakup, the Beatles remain the standard by which all rock is judged.

Sunshine of your Love

Words and Music by JACK BRUCE,
PETE BROWN and ERIC CLAPTON

I've been wait-ing so long to be where I'm go-ing in the sun-shine of your love.

D.S. al Coda

I'm

CODA

I've been wait - ing so long,

I've _ been wait - ing _ so long. _   I've _ been wait - ing so _ long

to _ be where _ I'm go - ing   in _ the sun - shine of _ your

love. _____

Cream • inducted 1993

They called themselves Cream, and that's just what they were—the three best British rock instrumentalists of the late sixties. Guitarist Eric Clapton, bassist Jack Bruce, and drummer Ginger Baker elevated musicianship and virtuosic prowess to a new level; Clapton's powerfully lyrical playing and expressive tone established him as the first "guitar hero."

Formed in the summer of 1966, Cream mixed original material with highly charged versions of blues standards from such masters as Robert Johnson and Muddy Waters. 1967's *Disraeli Gears*, Cream's second album, reflected the psychedelic atmosphere of the era, exemplified by Clapton's revolutionary use of the wha-wha pedal on "Tales of Brave Ulysses." Another highlight was "The Sunshine of Your Love," a definitive hard rock song that provided a model for hundreds of other bands. (Jack Bruce composed the immortal riff, while Clapton wrote the song's bridge.) 1968's *Wheels of Fire* captured examples of the lengthy improvisational jams that had become the band's trademark. Cream broke up later that year, having already established many of the basic musical conventions still practiced by rock groups worldwide.

The Twist

**Words and Music by
HANK BALLARD**

round and a-round and a -) Just, _____ just like this, ('round and a-round) come on,__ lit-tle

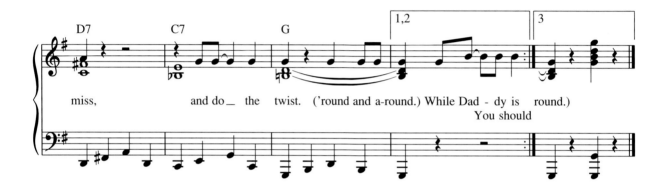

miss,   and do__ the twist. ('round and a-round.) While Dad - dy is   round.)
                                                                    You should

Hank Ballard • inducted 1990

When "The Twist" comes to mind, we tend to think of Chubby Checker, the performer who brought the song to the top of the pop charts not once, but twice, inciting an international dance craze. It's time to include Hank Ballard, the composer and original performer of "The Twist" in those collective memories. Ballard has other classics to his credit including "Finger Poppin' Time," "Let's Go, Let's Go, Let's Go," and his continuing saga of Annie: "Work with Me, Annie," "Annie Had A Baby," and "Annie's Aunt Fanny." The ribald lyrics of the "Annie" singles brought both huge sales and wide-scale radio bans of the records.

Ballard, with his group the Midnighters, recorded "The Twist" as the throwaway b-side to their 1958 hit single "Teardrops on My Letter." Two years later, Checker picked up on the forgotten flip side, taking his version to Number One. (It returned to the top spot in 1962.) Ballard may not have known it when he first brought the song to life, but he had created a rock and roll monster.

The Weight

By J.R. ROBERTSON

Slowly, with a beat

mf 1. I pulled in-to Naz-a-reth, was feel-ing 'bout half past dead, __
2.-5. *(See additional lyrics)*

I just need some place where I can lay my head. _____

Hey, Mis-ter, can you tell me where a man might find a bed.

Chorus

He just grinned and shook my hand, and 'no' was all he said. _ Take a load off Fan-ny,

Take a load for free.___ Take a load off Fan-ny. And___ you
put the load right on me.

Additional Lyrics

2. I picked up my bag, I went lookin' for a place to hide
   When I saw Carmen and the devil walkin' side by side
   I said, "Hey, Carmen, come on, let's go downtown."
   She said, "I gotta go, but my friend can stick around."
   (Chorus)

3. Go down, Miss Moses, there's nothing you can say
   It's just old Luke, and Luke's waitin' on the Judgement Day
   Well, Luke my friend, what about young Anna Lee?
   He said, "Do me a favor, son, won't you stay and keep Anna Lee Company."
   (Chorus)

4. Crazy Chester followed me and he caught me in the fog
   He said, "I'll fix your rack if you'll just jack my dog."
   I said, "Wait a minute, Chester, you know, I'm a peaceful man."
   He said, "That's okay, boy, won't you feed him when you can."
   (Chorus)

5. Catch a cannonball, now take me down the line
   My bag is sinkin' low and I do believe it's time
   To get back to Miss Fanny, you know she's the only one
   Who sent me here with her regards for everyone.
   (Chorus)

The Band • inducted 1994

After going electric in 1965, Bob Dylan needed an experienced back-up group to take out on the road. He hooked up with the Hawks, a Toronto quintet made up of four hard-rocking Canadians and a transplanted Arkansas native. After years of rigorous touring and subsequent informal recording with Dylan in their basement studio in Saugerties, New York, the now-unnamed quintet was ready to make its own music. Casually dubbed "the band" for some years, they took on the offhand name officially.

The Band's 1968 debut, *Music from Big Pink*, was a revelation: a soulful blend of rock and roll, gospel, country, and folk elements. "The Weight," by guitarist Robbie Robertson, became an instant classic. 1969's *The Band* (which included "The Night They Drove Old Dixie Down") surpassed *Big Pink* in commercial and critical impact. Despite their subsequent success, the original quintet decided to call it quits in 1976. The acclaimed rock documentary *The Last Waltz*, a film of the Band's final concert, was a fitting tribute to a landmark group.

Turn, Turn, Turn

Words from the Book of Ecclesiastes
Adaptation and Music by PETE SEEGER

gath - er   stones _____   to - geth - er. _____   To   ev - 'ry - thing   (turn,

turn,   turn)   there   is   a   sea - son   (turn,   turn,   turn)   and   a   time   for   ev - 'ry

pur - pose   un - der   heav - en.

A   time   of   love,   a   time   of   hate;   a   time   of
A   time   to   gain,   a   time   to   lose,   a   time   to

war,   a   time   of   peace;   a   time   you   may   em - brace,   a   time   to
bend,   a   time   to   sew;   a   time   to   love,   a   time   to   hate,   a   time   for

re - frain   from   em - brac - ing. _____   To   ev - 'ry -
peace   I   swear   it's   not   too   late. _____   To   ev - 'ry -

thing (turn, turn, turn) there is a sea-son (turn, turn, turn) And a

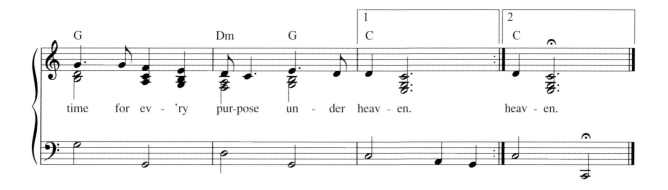

time for ev - 'ry pur-pose un - der heav - en. heav - en.

The Byrds • inducted 1991

The Byrds had an enormous influence on the folk-rock scene of the mid-sixties as well as on such contemporary superstars as Tom Petty and R.E.M. The original Byrds—Roger McGuinn, David Crosby, Gene Clark, Chris Hillman, and Michael Clarke—consciously mated the electric energy of the Beatles to the poetic visions of Bob Dylan. After defining folk rock on their 1965 hit version of Dylan's "Mr. Tambourine Man," the Byrds turned to another folk legend, Pete Seeger, for their follow-up. "Turn! Turn! Turn!," a Seeger adaptation of a biblical passage, also hit the Top Ten.

The Byrds continued to reach new heights, recording the monumental "Eight Miles High" and the albums *Younger Than Yesterday* and *Sweetheart of the Rodeo*. Distinct echoes of the Byrds could be heard in Crosby, Stills and Nash, the band Crosby co-formed in 1969 and subsequent Southern California groups like the Eagles. In the eighties, a whole new generation drew inspiration from the jangley twelve-string guitar parts and soaring vocal harmonies of the Byrds— a musical legacy that's now part of the fiber of rock and roll.

Tutti Frutti

Words and Music by RICHARD PENNIMAN
and D. LA BOSTRIE

gal,   her name's Sue,   She knows just what to do,___   I got a
gal,   her name's Dai - sy,   She al - most drives me cra - zy.   I got a

gal,   her name's Sue.   She knows just what to do. ___   I've
gal,   her name's Dai - sy,   she al - most drives me cra - zy.   She's a

been to the east,   I've been to the west,   but she's the gal __ I love the best. __ } Tut - ti
real gone cook-ie,   yes - sir - ree,   but pret-ty lit-tle Su-zy's the gal for me. __ }

fruit - ti   au rut-ti,   tut - ti frut-ti   au rut-ti,   tut - ti

frut-ti   au rut-ti,   tut - ti frut-ti   au rut-ti,   tut - ti

frut-ti   au   rut-ti,   a - bop-bop a-loom-op a - lop bop boom! I got a   lop bop boom!

Little Richard • inducted 1986

With the immortal words, "a wop bop a loo bop a wop bam boom," Little Richard burst into rock and roll history. 1955's "Tutti Frutti" was a declaration that the big beat was here to stay and that Richard Penniman had the voice, the energy, and attitude to get that message across. The songs he popularized are touchstones that have come to define an era: "Lucille," "Rip It Up," "Long Tall Sally," "Good Golly Miss Molly," among them. With the early work of Chuck Berry and Elvis Presley, these songs constitute the marrow of rock and roll. Little Richard's flamboyant presence and frantic performance style made him an instant legend. Behind the wild antics was a glorious voice soaked in gospel and rhythm & blues and an intense piano style that turned the instrument into a rock and roll tool long before electric guitars became the norm. Today, Little Richard—now a pop icon through his work on TV and film—is still the last word in rock and roll outrageousness.

Twist and Shout

Words and Music by BERT RUSSELL
and PHIL MEDLEY

You know you got me go - in' now, Just like I knew you would.
Come on and twist a lit - tle clos - er now, _ And let me know that you're _

mine.

Well, shake it up ba -

Ah   Ah   Ah   Ah _____

Shake it up ba -

Well, shake it, shake it, shake it, ba - by, now. _

Well, shake it, shake it, shake it, ba - by now. _   Ah

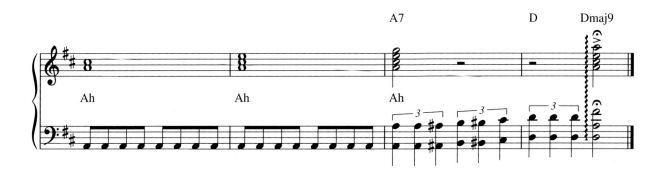

Isley Brothers • inducted 1992

The Isley Brothers have covered a lot of ground—from R&B to soul to funk—since they started recording in the late fifties. Ronnie, Kelley, and Rudolph first came to national prominence with "Shout," their debut single for RCA in 1959. The ultimate paean to revelry, "Shout" will be heard as long as mankind continues to throw parties. 1962's "Twist and Shout" nearly reaches the jubilant heights of its predecessor. The Isleys were favorites on the R&B circuit; in 1964 their backing band included Jimi Hendrix, who undoubtedly picked up a move or two from the brothers' legendary live act.

Signing with Motown in 1965, the Isleys cut the Holland-Dozier-Holland soul classic "This Old Heart of Mine." Four years later, the brothers modernized their sound by writing and producing the Sly Stone-influenced smash "It's Your Thing." Remaking their identity once again with the funk rock of "That Lady" and "Fight the Power," the Isleys began a fresh hit streak that took them through the seventies and eighties.

The Drifters • inducted 1988

No matter who sang lead for the group during its continual evolution—Clyde McPhatter, Ben E. King, Johnny Moore, Charlie Thomas, or Rudy Lewis—the Drifters were responsible for some of the most enchanting vocal hits of the fifties and early sixties. There are classics from each edition of the group: "Money Honey" with McPhatter; "There Goes My Baby," "This Magic Moment," and "Save the Last Dance for Me" with King; "Up on the Roof" and "On Broadway" with Lewis; "Sweets for My Sweet" with Thomas; and "Under the Boardwalk" with Moore, among them. The Drifters's greatest records were cut for Atlantic, using the finest behind-the-scenes craftsmen; among their producers were the team of Jerry Leiber and Mike Stoller, whose groundbreaking use of strings and Latin rhythms gave the early-sixties units their signature sound. Composers for the group included Burt Bacharach and the writing teams of Leiber and Stoller, Carole King and Gerry Goffin, and Doc Pomus and Mort Shuman.

Under the Boardwalk

**Words and Music by ARTIE RESNICK
and KENNY YOUNG**

Oh, when the sun beats down_ and burns the tar up-on the roof,_____
park you hear_ and hap-py sound of a car-ou-sel,_____

And your shoes get so hot you wish your tired feet_ were fire_____
You can al-most taste the hot - dogs and french - fries_____

_____ proof. Un - der the board - walk,_ down by the sea,_
they sell. Un - der the board - walk,_ down by the sea,_

_____ yeah, On a blan-ket with my ba - by's_____
_____ yeah, On a blan-ket with my ba - by's_____

Keep Me Hangin' On

Words and Music by EDDIE HOLLAND,
LAMONT DOZIER and BRIAN HOLLAND

Moderately

Set me free why don't _ cha ba - by; get out my life why don't cha _ ba - by,
Set me free why don't _ cha ba - by; let me be why don't cha _ ba - by,

'cause you don't _ real-ly love _ me. You just keep _ me hang - in' on. _____
'cause you don't _ real-ly love _ me. You just keep _ me hang - in' on. _____

You don't _ real-ly need _ me but you keep _ me hang - in' on. _____
You don't _ real-ly want _ me you just keep _ me hang - in' on. _____

Why do _ you keep a com-in' a - round _ play - ing with my heart? _____

Fmaj7   Esus   Bb/C

_ cha ba - by._ You claim _ you still _ care _ for me _ but your

F   C   Bb/C .

heart and soul needs to be free. _____ Now that _____ you've got _

F   C   Em/B   A

_____ your free - dom you wan-na still hold on to me. ___ Get out, _ get out -

Em/G   Em/D   Fmaj7   Esus   A

- ta my life and let me sleep at night, _____ 'cause you don't. real-ly love_

Em/G   Em/D   Fmaj7   Esus   A

_ me, you just keep _ me hang - in' on. _____ 'Cause you don't _ real-ly need_

me, _____ so _____ let me be, _____ set me free. _____

The Supremes • inducted 1988

The Supremes were the crown jewels of Berry Gordy's Motown empire. The epitome of all-girl groups, Diana Ross, Florence Ballard, and Mary Wilson had the looks, the moves, and the sound that catapulted them to international stardom. Diana Ross's lean, urgently affecting voice cushioned by Ballard and Wilson's harmonies became one of the signature sounds of the era. From 1964 to 1969, the Supremes scored twelve Number One hits, including "Where Did Our Love Go?," "Stop! In the Name of Love," "Baby Love," "You Keep Me Hangin' On," and "Someday We'll Be Together." Gordy showered the trio with the best that Motown's resources could provide, from choice material and production to high–profile publicity and prestigious live appearances. Ballard was replaced in 1967, the same year the trio was renamed "Diana Ross and the Supremes." At the end of 1969, with the group still enormously popular, Ross left to embark on a solo career. The group carried on with Wilson at the helm, but Ross's departure signaled the beginning of the end of Motown's golden age.